PAINTING ON PORCELAIN

Composition and Technique

DONY ALEXIEV

ANDRE DEUTSCH
ULISSEDITIONS

Painting on Porcelain: Composition and Technique. Copyright © 1989, 1994 by Dony Alexiev. All rights reserved. No part of this book may be reproduced in any form or by any electronic or mechanical means including information storage and retrieval systems without permission in writing from the publisher, except by a reviewer, who may quote brief passages in a review.

Original edition published in 1989 by Ulisséditions, Asnières, France, under the title *Motifs sur porcelaine: peindre et dessiner.*

Photos: Eric Morin
Cover: Piero Polato
Design: Mario Anesi
Filmsetting: RJ Informatique - 30133 Les Angles - France
Printed in Hong Kong - China by Colorkraft
English adaptation: John Tittensor

ISBN 0-233-98950-0

Contents

Author's preface 5

1. Chinese Beginnings
Historical background 6
A Choice of Shapes 10
Decoration 12
Hints on Technique 16
'Famille verte' 20
'Famille rose' 22

2. The Japanese Tradition
Historical background 27
A Choice of Shapes 30
Decoration 32

3. The East India Companies 34

4. Europe Cracks the Porcelain Code
Historical Background 38
The German Tradition: Meissen 49
The Secret Leaks Out 57
The French Manner: Sèvres 65
Sèvres: Shapes 74
Decoration 75
Little Boxes 79

Acknowledgements 80

Taste is shaped by the contemplation
of excellence, not of the commonplace.
                              GOETHE

Author's preface

The aim of this book is first and foremost to provide examples of landscapes, flowers and other common designs which can readily be used by those wishing to put their love of decorated porcelain into practice. This approach is backed up by an introduction to the most common porcelain pieces, with the aim of helping the learner to choose the designs most appropriate to each. It will then be up to him to go in greater depth into the technical and aesthetic questions raised by his choice of shapes and his stylistic preferences.

This emphasis on practice rather than theory may mean, for some readers, that my treatment of the discovery and development of porcelain techniques from the earliest times up until the 18th century will seem too short; but my aim, as I have already said, is to come to grips with the subject as directly as possible.

The reader may also wonder why I have opted for an overview that restricts itself to the factories of Meissen and Sèvres, given that these are only two among the vast crowd of manufacturers that came into being when porcelain first arrived in Europe.

We must not forget that there was no such thing as copyright in the 17th and 18th centuries and that as a result the porcelain industry of the time was marked by an uncontrolled interchange of ideas, forms and decorative designs. Thus a multitude of small German manufacturers - and even Vincennes and Sèvres at the beginning - imitated Meissen. However, from the mid-18th century onwards, everyone looked for inspiration to French shapes and decorative styles; some factories even went as far as to produce exact replicas of pieces produced by the leading manufacurers.

Since time immemorial art has been an international phenomenon and as such has been marked by a ongoing exchange of influences.

With this in mind I have included examples of work from a range of different cultures and periods for the learner to reproduce. Copying is certainly not an end in itself, but the old masters have a lot to teach us as we work our way towards a truly personal mode of expression.

1. Chinese Beginnings

Historical background

Ceramics is the overall term used for objects made of clay and given permanent form by firing. Earthenware, stoneware and porcelain represent different branches of this age-old marriage of earth and fire.
Porcelain, the most refined of all ceramic materials, contains two main ingredients: kaolin, a malleable white clay which melts when subjected to heat; and feldspar, a mineral which also melts when heated and which gives porcelain its characteristic translucence. Other minerals, such as quartz, are used as binders. Indispensable for the manufacture of true porcelain, kaolin takes its name from Kaoling ('high hill'),

the mountain in the Chinese province of Jiangxi which was the source of the first imports of this clay into Europe.

In China the art of pottery making dates from the neolithic period. Its development was closely linked to the production of bronze, which gave rise to advances in high-temperature firing methods. Although the exact dates remain uncertain, it was around 1250 BC that potters succeeded in using felspathic clays - and probably kaolin - to obtain the extremely hard chinas that we now call 'protoporcelains'.

The passing of time also brought improvements in the glazes, the vitreous coatings that make pottery impervious to liquids. The first lead-based glazes appeared some 2000 years ago. Around 200 AD a new pale green glaze was invented: combined with porcelain, this glaze would later give rise to celadon, which caused a sensation when it was first brought to Europe. This type of ware is still widely made and much appreciated by connoisseurs. The first true porcelain - pure white and translucent - made its appearance during the Tang Dynasty, between 600 and 800 AD. Initially it resembled a sort of white stoneware, but as the choice of ingredients gradually stabilized it became clear that this was a new and highly distinctive form of pottery.

At the same period iron oxide and copper oxide came into use as colourants. The browns and greens thus obtained made possible the first polychrome underglaze paintings of peonies, dragons and phoenixes. The Tang period was marked by the use of yellow, brown, green and blue glazes, which formed the basis of a style known as Sancai ('three colours').

The Sung Dynasty (960-1279) brought further progress at the technical level. The quality of the glazes and colourants improved and the decorative range increased accordingly, with fish, birds, fruit and flowers among the most widely-used designs.

The fall of the Sung Dynasty was followed by a period of great change. The Mongol invasion, begun in the north early in the 13th century, led to the establishment of the Yüan Dynasty (1276-1368) and to the impoverishment of the country as a whole. As a result the ceramics industry had to set its sights on foreign markets, which

This type of decoration was achieved either by painting in relief or by incising the design in the partly dried clay, the aim being to prevent the glazes from mixing with one another. Once the outline was complete, the colours - in this case greens and yellows - could be applied.

The dragon possesses a whole host of symbolic meanings. Here he represents Man in search of perfection: having freed himself from his watery prison, he sets out in pursuit of the fiery pearl that is his soul. The dragon also symbolizes the Emperor and is associated with rain and the notion of fertility.

The phoenix (*fong hoang*) is the symbol of the Empress and a sign of imminent good fortune.

This kind of underglaze design is created in two stages. Firstly, the outlines of the pattern must be drawn, using a 'crow quill' pen and a rich green. The design is then filled in with light green and the colours fixed by firing. The second stage consists of adding in the yellow background and, if necessary, retouching certain details of the green areas. A second firing, at a lower temperature than the first, concludes the process.

meant having to adapt its products to the tastes of different buyers. At the same time the sheer size of the Mongol empire, which stretched into Korea in the south and as far as Galicia, on the Polish-Russian border, in the west, aided the spread of Chinese porcelain. Since most trade took place by sea, it was the factories of the coastal provinces of the south that benefited most from this new state of affairs. However, the largest porcelain manufacturing centre during the Yüan Dynasty was at the inland city of Jingdezhen (also called King To Tchen), some 450 kilometres southwest of Shanghai; here, one factory was entirely devoted to meeting the needs of the Imperial Court, while countless smaller workshops fuelled the export trade.

It was at this time that cobalt oxide imported from the Near East - probably from Iran - was first used for underglaze painting. New designs produced in a more vigorous drawing style created a striking contrast with the now flawless white of the porcelain and led to the resounding success of 'Chinese blue and white'.

The defeat of the Mongols by nationalist forces in 1368 saw a truly Chinese dynasty - the Ming - take power and remain in place until 1644. After an initial period of social and economic unrest, the manufacture of porcelain, which had been severely disrupted, resumed. The new regime gave the industry its full protection and Jingdezhen soon regained its former status.

The blue and white style reached its apogee at this time. In addition decorative techniques were enriched by the introduction of on-glaze colours that could be fired at low temperatures; the use of the Wucai or 'five colours' - in fact made up of six or seven colours - led to the appearance of a new style called Famille verte ('green ware')*. A decline in the power of the Ming Dynasty from the late 16th century onwards, caused by internal political problems and later by revolts, resulted in the occupation of China by the Manchus. Jingdezhen was thrown into chaos: the majority of the workshops were destroyed and the painters and pottery-makers fled.

However, the Qing Dynasty (1644-1911) established by the Manchus set itself the task of getting the porcelain industry back on its feet, under the direction of efficient and energetic overseers. It was thanks to this policy that the successive reigns of Kangxi (1662-1722), Yonzheng (1723-1735) and Qianlong (1736-1796) - a period marked by the meeting of technical and artistic perfection - came to represent the golden age of Chinese porcelain-making. A crucial factor was the introduction into China by Jesuit missionnaries, probably at the end of the Kangxi period, of a rose-coloured pigment invented by the 17th-century German physician Andreas Cassius. The 'purple of Cassius' was immediately taken up by porcelain painters and quickly assumed a dominant role in the preparation of their colours; the porcelain of the time bears the overall name of Famille rose ('rose family').

The French names given to the different Chinese porcelain 'families' in the 19th century are still widely used in English.

Rim of a famille rose dish. The cartouche - the peony design enclosed within its 'frame' - is used six times in all on the dish. As is the case here, the pattern between the cartouches often varies, but there is nothing to prevent you from making it uniform.

A Choice of Shapes

Chinese porcelain is justifiably renowned for the restraint and elegance of its shapes. The earliest known pieces are of an extreme simplicity, but technical advances and continuous experimentation led to the creation of a rich and varied repertoire.

The number of forms presented in this book is fairly restricted and the choice has been influenced to a certain extent by the types of pieces readily available in the shops. Study the drawings opposite carefully: learning to identify the characteristic line of Chinese porcelain objects will help considerably when it comes to choosing the right kind of decoration for a particular piece. The range of shapes includes elegant broad-bellied vases with wide necks; 'egg-shaped', square and octagonal lidded recipients; perfume bottles; tea bowls; bowls and dishes for rice or meat; and a variety of plates.

The plates fall into categories defined according to the type of rim: this can be smooth and continuous or scalloped in a simple, regular manner which imitates in a stylized way the petals of the chrysanthemum; on the third type of rim the scalloping is replaced by accolades.

The decoration of a vase is usually carried out panel by panel, except in the case of the ovoid, or egg-shaped pieces: here the main subject is painted on the belly of the vase and the neck, shoulder and base are decorated with stylized or geometrical patterns. The rims and bottoms of the plates are sometimes very richly decorated and there are examples of plates whose rim bears no less than seven different border designs.

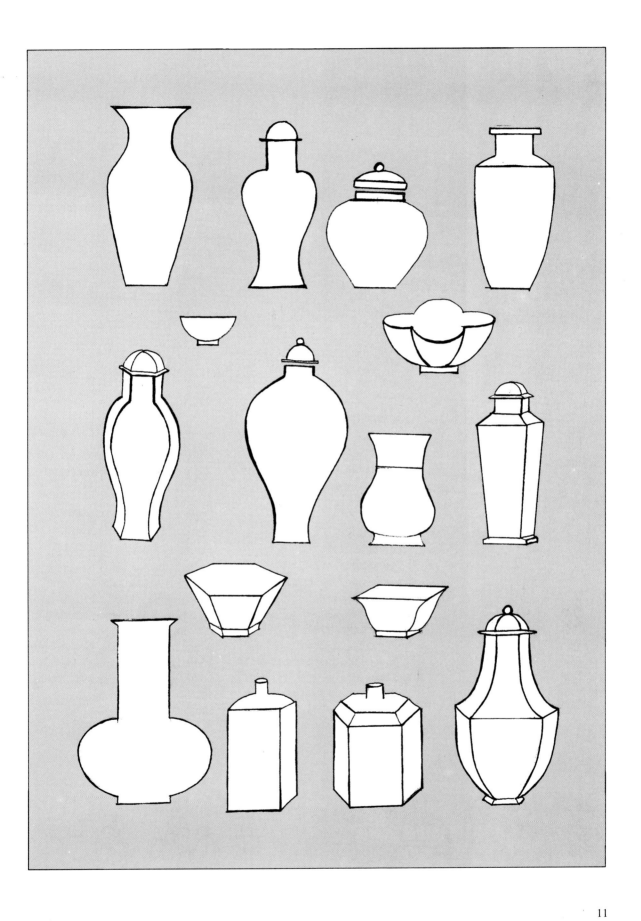

Decoration

Chinese painting on porcelain is imbued with a respect for tradition and for the work of the country's great painters.

The patterns, colours and compositions are taken directly from those used for painting on silk and paper. While it is true that ancient China had no art schools in our sense of the term, from the 16th century onwards the learner had access to comprehensive and highly detailed manuals; these explained the different techniques and backed up their advice with a multitude of pictorial examples taken from the work of the masters. Wood engraving, a widespread art form in China, also had a considerable influence on porcelain decoration, whose practitioners often went to woodcuts in search of their subjects.

On the technical level two main styles stand out. The first opts for a relatively detailed approach and makes considerable use of patterns clearly outlined in the Chinese ink-drawing tradition. The second, which made its appearance around 1630, is called in Chinese the 'no bones' style; the name is due to the absence of ink-drawing, the subjects being treated exclusively in terms of colour.

Whatever the style, the skill that went into the decoration of Chinese porcelain pieces was remarkable. The work was entrusted either to gifted artists or, in the case of mass production, to craftsmen who had mastered a particular subject or detail by painting it over and over again. In addition the legacy of the past was ever-present: drawing endlessly on the works, techniques and sensibility of the masters, the decorators created an enormous range of scenes and designs. Certain pieces are marked by a rigorous simplicity, others by a complexity which allies an extraordinarily precise touch to an all-round virtuosity; still others bear scenes portraying a whole host of human figures.

The richness of the decorative repertoire is as subtle as it is varied. To give but one example, the 'simplicity' of Chinese calligraphy - especially when used on its own - is much more apparent than real. The visual structure of the ideograms, the individual artist's touch and the script chosen can raise a calligraphic motif - vertical lines of characters expressing good wishes or delicately poetic sentiments - to the status of a work of art in its

own right. Calligraphy is also found in the company of figurative decoration, as is the case in the tradition of painting on paper or silk.

Nature was an unfailing source of inspiration. Not only do plants, trees, flowers, insects and birds play a particularly important role, each is depicted via a specific artistic language. Landscapes are another of the timeless themes used here: sometimes enlivened by the presence of fishermen, woodcutters or peasants going about their daily tasks, they also provide a perfect setting for the peregrinations of philosophers, sages and Taoist saints.

In certain cases the human element becomes dominant and decorated porcelain pieces show us battles, tournaments, religious ceremonies and historical or legendary events. In a lighter vein, we find representations of dances, festivals and children at play - not to mention beautiful, elegantly-clad women playing the flute or the zither or strolling in incomparable gardens.

The seemingly limitless imagination of these artists is nothing short of dazzling. But as the décors became ever more complex, as the scale of the pieces and their decoration came to cover the whole range from the miniature to the frankly gigantic, the art-form fell victim to its own over-elaborateness. In addition, in their attempts to imitate the look of other materials - wood or brocade, for example - the porcelain painters lost control of their colours. At the same time, a monotony due to the over-use of certain highly elaborate designs set in and by the end of the 18th century Chinese porcelain had gone into a period of marked aesthetic decline.

These butterflies fluttering around the branch of a flowering tree are a modern adaptation of a design on a Kangxi bowl. Note the contrast between the 'no bones' style used for the branch and the much more precise definition of the butterflies; this latter approach is closely related to the meticulously detailed work that characterizes the *gongbi* style.

Ming dynasty bowl decorated by Wan Li (1573-1620). The medallions of flowers and fruit are in the *doucay* style. The delicate underglaze outlines are in blue; after firing the design is filled in with iron red, yellow and green.

Hints on Technique

The designs suggested here are very simple and are a useful way of getting to know the basic techniques.

- Firstly, trace the designs or draw them freehand using a wax pencil. The outline thus produced should be as light as possible.

- The colour for your outline drawing - to be effected with a 'crow quill' pen - should be prepared as follows:

• Porcelain paints come in powder form. Place a little dark blue on the palette (a grinding glass or glazed tile).

• Add caster sugar (one sixth of the quantity of paint) and water, then blend with a palette knife until you obtain a smooth, manageable mixture.

• Draw several lines with your crow quill pen on a trial surface, allow them to dry for a few minutes, then test them by rubbing

with your finger. If the line rubs out or blurs, your mix needs more sugar.

- For the filling-in, prepare your paints step by step, as follows:
• Place the required amount of paint powder on the palette, add turpentine and mix with a circular motion, from the edge inwards. Once the paste is really smooth, add a little mixing oil (fat oil of turpentine) until the mixture flows well.
• Load your brush with the necessary amount of paint and apply the colour to the appropriate areas. Above all, remember that the red and the yellow go perfectly well side by side, but must not be mixed or painted one on top of the other. In the case of the litchis (this page, top right), the red has been largely 'swallowed up' by the underlying yellow. A way of avoiding this that sometimes works is to saturate your iron red by adding a little red violet.

Certain fruits, flowers, trees and animals that recur frequently in Chinese porcelain decoration have a precise symbolic significance. The design in the top and bottom right-hand corners of the page opposite, for example, shows the Chinese peach, known as the t'ao. According to Taoist doctrine, to eat this peach is to gain immortality - perhaps because the tree is said to bear fruit only once every three thousand years! The t'ao is also the emblem of marriage.

Qing Dynasty tea bowl decorated by Yong Zheng (1723-1735). The blue underglaze outline is in the *doucay* style, using yellow, red, a saturated red, and green. The fruits - the Buddha's hand lemon, the litchi and the pomegranate - are called collectively the Three Blessings and symbolize happiness, long life and fertility.

The convulvulus design below is in the same style, but is taken from a different piece.

Another version of the Three Blessings groups the *t'ao* with the pomegranate and the Buddha's hand lemon.

Among the conventional elements used in porcelain decoration were a variety of specifically Buddhist symbols. The following list corresponds to the numbered examples shown below.

1. The wheel, symbol of Buddhist teachings and of the transmigration of the soul, at death, from one body to another.
2. The mystical knot, symbol of long life.
3. The fish, symbol of fertility.
4. The sacred vase containing Amrita, the elixir of life.
5. The lotus, symbol of purity.
6. The canopy, symbol of the emperor.
7. The parasol, symbol of dignity.
8. The shell, symbol of the voice of Buddha.

'FAMILLE VERTE'

Kangxi Period (1662-1722)

The famille verte ('green family') is so called because of the dominant role of various shades of green in the decoration. The range of green enamel colours used goes from very light and transparent to dark and heavily saturated. The design was painted on the initial overall glaze after firing ; the thickness of application varied according to the tonal effect sought by the artist, and you can feel the raised (or 'relief') paint areas by running your finger over the surface.

The colour range also included yellow, a blue that often had a purplish tinge to it, and a manganese brown for the outlines. Black was used for drawing or colouring hair. However, the black and iron red used are not enamel colours; they are simply coloured paints and as such have a matt finish and create no relief on the glaze.

The same period saw the appearance of the famille noire ('black family'). The overall background was black, but certain parts of it were left white by masking and the design was subsequently painted on to these areas. In this way the artist was able to choose colour schemes that would take maximum advantage of the contrast provided by the background.

Other backgrounds using different

yellows and greens were also used. In addition, designs picked out in gold began to appear, especially on pieces providing a black enamelled background.

The relief decoration of the famille verte plate shown on the opposite page incorporates green enamel colours of various shades. If you want to try this technique, you will

need to buy either a specific type of coloured glaze or a special additive that you will add to your ordinary porcelain paints. This latter comes in the form of a white powder, but does not modify the colours.

The two methods are as follows:

1. Coloured enamels Dissolve the enamel colour with turpentine and add a drop or two of mixing oil. The aim is to produce a very liquid enamel that can be painted on quickly with a fine, long-headed brush.

2. Paint mixture Prepare a fifty-fifty mix of porcelain paint and powder additive (see above), using turpentine and mixing oil to obtain a good liquid consistency. And don't forget: the additive cannot be used with iron red and black.

The introduction of purple of Cassius into porcelain decoration (see p.9), led to a transitional 'green-pink' period. The border design shown below is an example. Here, as in the illustrations above, the cartouche surrounding the central flower design is fruit-shaped, but the outlines of various leaves were also sometimes used.

'FAMILLE ROSE'

From 1722 to the present day

Around 1720 a new colour came on the scene in Chinese porcelain decoration. The arrival in China of purple of Cassius (see p.9) made possible a whole group of new shades going from light pink to rich ruby. Another new product, white arsenic, could also be added in varying quantities and opened the way to the creation of a virtually unlimited range of tints of pink and other colours. After a period of trial and error, the porcelain artists of the time mastered the harmonious use of this new palette, giving pride of place to the delicate pinks. The famille rose ('rose family') style is notable for the meticulousness and technical skill of its practitioners and for the richness of their designs.

The bats that often occur in Chinese porcelain painting are a symbol of happiness and good fortune.

Hints on technique
For the Chinese peaches (*t'ao*) on this plate the artist has used yellow and carmine tinged with purple; these three colours are compatible. Each peach should be completed before moving on to the next ; as you finish each one, give it a uniform texture by 'pouncing' - dabbing lightly all over with a sponge or a special brush. Then remove all smudges, smears and runs.

Hints on technique
For the rim design shown in the photos above, the paint has been prepared in a specific way. Firstly, the powder is mixed with a very small quantity of mixing oil, so as to give a dryish and almost matt paste. Then a drop of clove oil is added and the mix is diluted with turpentine until it becomes liquid enough to use. If you want to add other colours, this layer will have to be fired first.

2. The Japanese Tradition

Historical Background

Strange as it may seem, the art of making porcelain came to Japan from elsewhere - and there is no shortage of stories concerning its arrival.

One version has it that a certain Gorodayu Go Shonzui, whose origins remain unknown, had worked at Jingdezhen in China (see pp. 8-9); once having learnt the secrets of the trade, he brought them with him to Japan. No trace has been found of the porcelain workshop he is supposed to have set up in 1511, somewhere near Arita.

According to another traditional account, the first manufacturer of porcelain in Japan was Takahari Goroshichi, a Korean or Chinese potter. He too is said to have worked in the Arita region.

A third and relatively detailed version opts unequivocally for a Korean founding father. At the end of the 16th century low-born Japanese military leader Hideyoshi, named as regent by the emperor, decided to conquer China and opened hostilities by sending his army into Korea. Things went less well than expected and the Japanese forces finally had to withdraw in 1598, but the nobleman and military leader Naoshige Nabeshima is said to have brought back with him several Korean potters, with the intention of establishing a ceramics industry in the province he ruled. One of these potters, Ri Sampei, whose historical existence is beyond doubt, set up a workshop at Arita - and some time later came upon deposits of porcelain clay at Hizen, not far away. This discovery of kaolin in 1616 is taken as marking the beginnings of the porcelain industry in Japan. Arita had all the natural and other advantages required for the success of such a venture: not only was the area rich in firewood and water-power, it turned out to be the sole source of kaolin in the entire country. In addition, the nearby port of Imari facilitated the export of porcelain to other provinces and abroad - to the extent that 'Imari' became the generic name for Japanese porcelain all over the world.

Nabeshima took steps to ensure that the new industry should prosper without incurring an excessive deforestation of the province. The number of workshops in the area was limited to 155. The best-known of them were those of Ri Sampei, situated in the town of Arita; of the Korean, Shinkai Soden, in the countryside

Kakiemon design

The Nabeshima factory continues to produce porcelain of the finest quality. The decoration of this plate is inspired by a Nabeshima pattern.
Hints on technique: Cover the areas of the flowers, the leaves and the the wheel with masking fluid and pounce the coloured backgrounds with a brush or sponge. Remove the masking fluid before firing.

nearby; and of Sakaida Kakiemon, at Nangawara-Yama. In about 1660 the Nabeshima family set up its own factory to meet the needs of its Court and to make presents for the Shogun and various feudal princes.

Without exception these workshops functioned on a cottage-industry scale and even the Nabeshima concern employed only some thirty workers. This situation remained unchanged until the end of the 19th century.

Japan thus presents a marked contrast with China, where in the 18th century the town of Jingdezhen possessed 3000 kilns and a million inhabitants, all of whom earned their living in the porcelain industry.

The same divergence of approach could be seen in the methods of production: in China specialization and the division of labour were the order of the day within the workshops and it seems that the production line was invented at Jingdezhen. In Japan, on the other hand, individual workshops undertook specific tasks. At Arita, for example, 'Painters' Alley' was so called because the sixteen workshops specializing in painted glazes were situated there. The output of the factories was brought to these workshops for decoration. The secrets of glazing and painting were jealously guarded by each artist and a porcelain painter had the right to divulge his personal techniques solely to his eldest son. If he had no sons he could pass the secrets on to one of his daughters - but if she married her husband had to be a porcelain painter. When fire destroyed the painting workshops at Arita in 1928, these occupational traditions perished with them.

The store set by the art of making, glazing and painting porcelain is amply illustrated by the history of Soeda Kisaemon, better known as Kakiemon. Although he was born a commoner, the Nabeshima family granted him the title of *teakiyari* out of respect for his mastery of the making of high quality celadon. This meant that he had the same considerable status as a samourai.

Naturally enough, the first porcelain painters in Japan were influenced by Chinese methods and approaches and their work was initially in the 'blue and white' mode. At first the results were disappointing, Japanese cobalt being of inferior quality. Things improved with the importation of cobalt from China, but tradition has it that the real stimulus to on-glaze painting came with the arrival of Chinese painters fleeing the victorious Manchu invaders in 1644. As with the 'history' of the introduction of porcelain to Japan, the accuracy of this account remains uncertain.

One thing is sure, however: the political and military upheavals in China had marked repercussions. The local manufacture of porcelain came to a virtual halt and foreign merchants began to look to Japan to fill their orders; the effect was a dramatic growth in output and the spread of the Japanese article throughout the world.

The great majority of the workshops served the local and export markets, but there remained a few whose goals were not exclusively commercial. At the Nabeshima factory, for example, the emphasis was first and foremost on quality - but even so, the low level of profitability obliged the proprietors to produce a parallel range of pieces of a cheaper, more readily saleable type.

Porcelain factories enjoying the protection of noble families sprang up from time to time in other provinces and some would have their brief moment of glory during the 18th and 19th centuries. Exportation meant that Japanese porcelain, like the Chinese before it, gained world-wide renown. At the beginning of the 18th century it had a marked influence on the beginnings of porcelain-making in Europe.

Detail of an Imari design.
Hints on technique The painting in gold is added after the firing of the coloured background. The firing temperature of the gold should not exceed 700° C.

KEY NAMES

Arita: Town on the island of Kyushu, in southern Japan. Site of the country's first porcelain workshops.

Ri Sampei: 17th century Korean potter, credited with the introduction of porcelain to Japan and the discovery of kaolin at Hizen in 1616.

Nabeshima: Japanese nobleman, founder of a major porcelain factory in the 17th century.

Design in the Imari style
Hints on technique The blue leaves and stems do not have to be outlined with a pen, as this will be done in gold after firing. Draw the other leaves in gold at the same time, leaving part of the inside area white. The outlines and leaf-veins in red will be added after firing.

A Choice of Shapes

The introduction of porcelain into Japan came at a time that was particularly favorable to its rapid development. It also brought about a radical change in the Japanese conception of art. The local tradition as regards objects in everyday use was one of extreme simplicity and showed the influence of Zen Buddhism and of the tea ceremony, an unvarying ritual organized down to the last tiny detail.

The Korean potters who got the making of porcelain under way in Japan brought with them, naturally enough, a Korean style which had a marked effect at the beginning. In 1641 Dutch traders, who did not have the right to enter Japan, set up shop on the artificial island of Deshima, expressly created for them in Nagasaki harbour. The manufacturing centre of Arita was not far away and the quantities of Chinese porcelain brought in by the Dutch influenced the local style.

China, however, soon entered on a period of political chaos (see p.9) and could no longer meet the orders placed by overseas traders. The Japanese product was there to fill the breach, but this meant adapting to foreign tastes and expanding the range of shapes on offer. Nevertheless, towards the end of the 17th century specifically Japanese shapes were making their appearance, certain of them marked by the use of angles and facets.

This new indigenous style also reflected the Japanese passion for nature, which found expression in plates and bowls resembling flowers and later gave rise to the use of applied reliefs: blossom branches, for example, were added to a variety of pieces. This innovation met with such success that it was at once taken up by European manufacturers.

The criss-crossing of influences went on apace. Japanese porcelain had already drawn extensively on Chinese models - and now the Chinese began to look for inspiration to Japan, whose shapes and decorative styles had come to enjoy enormous prestige as well as a considerable slice of the market. Two centuries later we occidentals are more than ever under the spell of Japanese aesthetics. Fortunately a variety of suitable pieces can be found fairly easily and the western porcelain artist who wants to try out Japanese-style decoration can work either with celadon or the more common white porcelain.

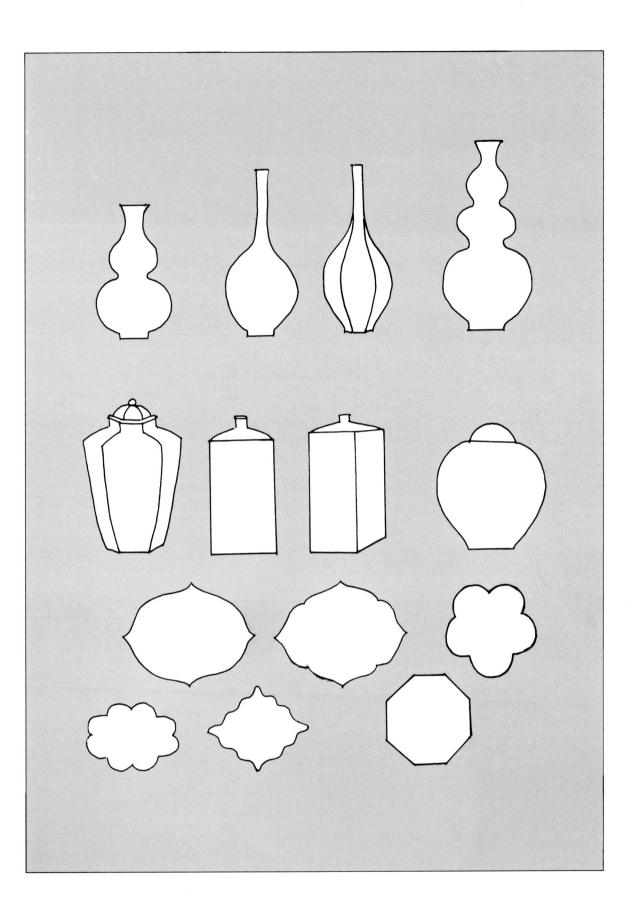

Decoration

In their gradual evolution towards a distinctive style, the approaches to porcelain decoration in Japanese workshops underwent the same influences and the same stages of development as the shapes of the articles produced.

As Chinese blue and white had already reached its apogee when porcelain making started in Japan, it is hardly surprising that the first Japanese porcelain painters opted for the use of underglaze cobalt blue. When China went into a period of upheaval and Japanese manufacturers had to cope with the enormous demand coming from Europe and the Islamic countries, blue remained the sole colour used, although it was sometimes set off by dark brown manganese outlines. The basic method divided the piece into broad and narrow bands: the former were decorated either with a figurative design or stylized plant shapes, while the latter were given over to geometrical patterns or flowery foliage in a stylized and symmetrical form.

The Kakiemon style is among the best-known of oriental porcelain decorative approaches and owes its name to a family which has been making porcelain in Japan for thirteen generations (see p.28). In the 18th century the Kakiemono workshop pioneered underglaze painting in Japan. Their style is characterized by the predominance of clear blue enamel and an iron red so delicate as to verge on the orange. Sometimes these colours are accompanied by a bluish green, a crisp grass-green and a pale yellow. The use of gold was very sparing. The designs used are for the most part plants and animals; landscapes and human figures are rare. Conceived without reference to the Chinese model, Kakiemon decoration is typically Japanese and manages to remain personal and spontaneous in spite of its stylized character.

The brocade style is also called 'Imari', after the port from which the output of the Arita workshops was exported to Europe and elsewhere. Brightly coloured, richly ornamented and shamelessly overloaded with gold, this style matched perfectly the baroque tastes prevalent in Europe, where it was a runaway success. The style was applied to all sorts of pieces, some of which - the vases in particular - were of impressive dimensions. Sumptuous and gaudy, the approach was dominated by three colours: cobalt blue (for the enamel), iron red and gold. It should be said, however, that certain pieces show a much more varied and subtle use of colour.

Imari patterns were executed with a minute attention to detail. The subject matter included flowers, trees, birds, butterflies, landscapes, animals and traditional and

Imitation brocade in the Imari style

Imitations of Chinese blue and white designs

Above: Imari red and gold border pattern

Left: In Asia the tiger is the king of the beasts. We note in this example the disproportionate length of the tail; this exaggeration is characteristic of the Japanese approach to tigers and birds and is regarded as highly decorative.

contemporary scenes - in other words the main decorative themes that we have already noted in the Chinese context. This similarity is hardly surprising, the two civilizations having known since the earliest times a geographical and cultural proximity that entailed a sharing of fundamental artistic resources: not only of the same signs, symbols and mythical creatures, but also of the same general aesthetic orientation.

In Japan, as in China, the fine and applied arts were closely related and artistic practice was underpinned by the use of precise and highly detailed technical manuals. The work of the great Japanese painters found its highest expression in a distinctively non-symmetrical approach to composition; this carried over into the decoration of porcelain, where a striking use of empty or near-empty space has the effect of enhancing the subject while imparting an atmosphere of harmony and serenity to the work as a whole.

KEY WORDS

Imari: Term loosely used for Japanese export porcelain.
Zen Buddhism: Japanese adaptation of 'ch'an' Buddhism, introduced from China at the end of the 12th century. Zen had a marked impact on all subsequent Japanese art forms.
Kakiemon: Creator of high-quality celadon in the 17th century and founder of a porcelain factory still in existence.

The Imari style found its imitators in China and the cycle of influences continues: this western plate reproduces a Chinese version of an Imari pattern.

3. The East India Companies

Men have always responded to the lure of the unknown, even when this meant traversing enormous distances; and although there is no way of dating exactly the first contacts between Europe and the Far East, it is certain that trading links were established in very early times.

We know, for example, that in the 4th century AD the Romans were already great admirers of the delicate fabrics produced in Serica, a name which means 'the country of silk' - China, in other words. For several centuries silk constituted the major single item of trade between the two great empires. It was transported overland from China via India, and changed hands where the respective trading caravans met on the banks of the Syr Darya, in Kazakhstan. However, parts of the overland silk route could be extremely dangerous and sometimes, in the interests of safety, the merchandise had to be moved by sea. During the Tang Dynasty (618-907) maritime trading activity was such that the shipping office of Canton took charge of the silk export traffic and drew up a system of taxes.

In 1275, having crossed Asia and reached China via Mongolia, Marco Polo arrived in Peking, where he spent 16 years as a high-ranking official at the court of

Kubla Khan. In his memoirs, written after his return to his native Venice in 1295, he spoke enthusiastically of a marvellous new ceramic material, unknown in the West. If we can believe the legend, a white porcelain vase now belonging to the basilica of San Marco in Venice was brought to Europe by the explorer-diplomat in person.

A century or so later, at the head of a dozen sea-going junks and some 20 000 men, the great Chinese explorer, Zheng He (1371-1435) led several expeditions into the unknown; soon China had become a diplomatic and commercial force to be reckoned with over an area embracing the Indian Ocean, Persia and Arabia. Porcelain naturally figured in the range of goods offered by Chinese traders and eventually became the main export item.

In 1497 the Portugese explorer Vasco da Gama discovered the route to India via the Cape of Good Hope and after a period of local resistance Portugal succeeded in establishing trading posts at Malacca, in Malaysia, and Canton. Later the Chinese ceded the island of Macao to Portugal as a trading centre. In these eastern ports the Portugese had occasional contacts with traders from Japan, a country of which Europeans remained totally ignorant until 1542, when a Chinese junk with three Portuguese aboard ran aground on the island of Tanagashima. The opening of trade relations between Japan and Macao was the immediate result. The discovery of the Philippines by the Spanish explorer Ferdinand Magellan in 1521 was quickly followed by colonization. This led to trading contacts with Japan, where Jesuit missionaries arrived hot on the heels of the merchants and succeeded in making numerous converts. The new religion, however, was not to the taste of the Japanese authorities, who asked the missionaries several times to leave; when they failed to do so, they were expelled and westerners were henceforth personae non gratae in Japan. Nonetheless, other countries continued to seek a place for themselves in the Asian markets. Despite continued opposition from Spain, in 1606 a group of energetic and efficient Dutch businessmen founded their country's East India Company. In 1641 Holland received Japanese permission to set up a trading post on the island of Deshima, in Nagasaki harbour. The British, under Elizabeth I, had founded their own East India Company a little before the Dutch; they set up shop in Canton and trade was so vigorous that English soon became the main language of business between China and the various European countries. Meanwhile, in France, the efforts of Henri IV and his son and heir Louis XIII to organize sea trade with the 'East Indies' were less successful. The first French trading post in Canton was not established until 1698 - and then the company went bankrupt. However, the replacement venture begun in 1718

soon gave France a major role in oriental trade.

Chinese porcelain had been an export item since the Tang Dynasty. The famous green celadon of the Sung Dynasty, followed later by blue and white porcelain, circulated widely in the Indian Ocean region and was even more appreciated in the Near East, but pieces arrived only haphazardly in Europe. Porcelain was so rare in Europe at the end of the Middle Ages and the beginning of the Renaissance that it was not to be found outside of royal collections. The respect in which it was held at this time can be gauged by the elaborateness of the bronze and silver mounts that the proud owners commissioned for their pieces. Indeed, so mysterious did this exotic substance seem to Europeans that they often regarded it as possessing magical properties. In the course of the 17th century ships of the various East India companies began to arrive in the major European ports with cargoes made up exclusively of porcelain. A wave of enthusiasm for things oriental swept the Continent and almost without exception the great families ordered pieces bearing their coats of arms. Table settings in porcelain became the norm and the custom arose of ordering pieces copied directly from contemporary objects made of glazed earthenware, silver or gold. The Chinese revealed a considerable gift when it came to producing copies and were also able, within limits, to adapt western engravings and paintings. This explains the existence of East India Company porcelain pieces decorated with non-oriental designs of a religious, mythological or romantic character.

The passion for things Chinese and Japanese in Europe lasted until the opening years of the 19th century, when it was supplanted by neo-classicism.

KEY NAMES

East India Companies: Companies established by various European countries to trade with India and the East.
Serica: 'Land of Silk': name used by the Romans to designate China.
Marco Polo: Venetian explorer (1254-1324) . Lived for 16 years in China and is reputed to have brought the first samples of porcelain to Europe.
Zheng He: Chinese explorer (1371-1435) whose expeditions into Arabia, the Indian Ocean region and elsewhere made porcelain his country's main export.
Deshima: Artificial island created by the Japanese in Nagasaki harbour as a base for trade with Europe.

4. Europe Cracks the Porcelain Code

Historical Background

Up until the 16th century objects made of porcelain were almost exclusively the privilege of kings and princes. These pieces had either been received as gifts from oriental potentates or acquired from travellers or traders. In the latter case the distances and dangers involved in the transport of the pieces from China made them prohibitively expensive. The rarity of porcelain and the aura of mystery surrounding it quickly gave rise to a series of contemporary myths. It was said, for example, that porcelain would change its appearance and even break into pieces if it came into contact with a poison; at the very least it was regarded as a protection against certain illnesses. These ideas are coloured by a belief in magic which no longer holds true, yet they contained an element of truth, for the hardness and imperviousness of porcelain kept at bay the germs which often lay hidden in the networks of cracks covering traditional glazed earthenware.

Porcelain became a near-obsession for certain collectors in the 17th and 18th centuries, notably the Prince de Condé in France: he was the patron of the factory established in 1725 at Chantilly and the possessor of magnificent collection of European and Japanese pieces. Augustus the Strong, Elector of Saxony, was another victim of the 'porcelain sickness', as it was called; he initiated the search for raw materials that led to the eventual establishment of the Meissen works, near Dresden, and built up a collection which still ranks among the finest in the world. Regular arrivals of cargoes from the Far East only added fuel to the flames. In one two-month period in 1671 Louis XVI of France treated himself to pieces to the value of £9000, no mean sum at the time. His example was not wasted on his successor Louis XV, whose porcelain budget ran around £500 000 per annum. The nobility, who sought to imitate their rulers by acquiring porcelain dinner services, were in turn imitated by the rising bourgeoisie. But if porcelain brought prestige, its purchase entailed an enormous loss of hard currency and in all the porcelain-buying countries experts were set the task of breaking the manufacturing code. This line of research had in fact been pursued, unsuccessfully, ever since Marco Polo returned to Europe singing the praises of porcelain in 1295. According to his account, the secret of the characteristic whiteness and translucence lay in leaving the clays exposed to air and light for between 30 and 40 years.

Three centuries later Guido Panciroli, an Italian judicial expert

Meissen designs. The three cartouches show trading scenes.

Chinese-style Meissen decoration.

work in Florence, but the end-product was a 'soft paste', whereas true porcelain is described as 'hard-paste'. Unfortunately there was no real follow-up to this interesting discovery and production stopped with Francesco de Medici's death in 1587. Medici 'porcelain' is now extremely rare and only a handful of museums in London, Florence, Paris and New York possess examples.

It was to be a hundred years before any fruitful research got under way again, this time in France. In 1673 a royal patent authorized Louis Poterat, of Rouen - and not long afterwards a factory at Saint-Cloud, near Paris - to make what was described as 'true porcelain'. Despite the precautions taken to protect the trade secrets involved, factories began to multiply in France - but once again, the porcelain in question was a 'soft paste', made from a clay rich in lime to which was added a 'frit' composed of ground potassium, alum, gypsum and other ceramic raw materials. Fired at a lower temperature, this style of porcelain uses a highly fusible lead-based glaze which can impart a stunning luminosity to the decorative elements. Unfortunately the undeniable artistic qualities of 'soft-paste' have to be weighed against some major shortcomings: the pieces are fragile, the glaze scratches easily and a high proportion of failures during the firing raises problems of profitability.

What was lacking in these early versions was the basic material - kaolin - and no analysis of oriental pieces succeeded in breaking the code. It seems that the 'discovery' of porcelain-making in Europe came about by chance. Johann Friedrich Böttger, an apprentice chemist in a Berlin pharmacy, was

with a wide but sometimes shaky grasp of non-legal matters, passed on a recipe going back, in theory at least, to ancient times: porcelain clay was to be obtained by mixing eggshells, lobster-shells and 'other similar materials' with gypsum and burying the result for 80 years. Panciroli at least had the good sense to remind his readers to show their children and grandchildren exactly where the precious mixture was to be found… As impatient as ever, Panciroli's countrymen carried out various experiments in the course of the 16th century, at the royal courts of Pesaro, Turin and Ferrara. But to no avail. In Venice a white translucent substance was obtained, but this was an opaline or 'milk-glass' and not a true porcelain. In the second half of the century, Francesco de Medici, renowned for his scientific interests, set his researchers to

Meissen designs. The landscapes were often inspired by the works of Flemish painters.

Stylized flowers from the Herend factory in Hungary.

friendly with the industrial chemist Johann Kunckel and a group of alchemists and was involved in their quest for the philosopher's stone, reputed to be capable of changing base metals into gold. When the rumour that Böttger could make gold reached Wilhelm of Prussia, the king had him put in prison as a way of persuading him to reveal his secrets. A strange and resourceful personage, Böttger escaped and took refuge in Saxony; faced with the Prussian demand for Böttger's extradition, Augustus the Strong, Elector of Saxony, chose to shut up his valuable prize in the castle of Koenigsberg and provide him with all the money, facilities and manpower he needed to further his researches.

Obviously the search for the philosopher's stone was a blind alley and Böttger would have had some explaining to do had not von Tschirnhaus, the Elector's economic adviser, been struck by the young man's intelligence and asked him, in 1704, to assist in the experiments into porcelain-making he was directing. The results were not slow in coming and Böttger and von Tschirnaus had soon succeeded in turning out a fine dark red stoneware.

After the death of von Tschirnaus in 1708, Böttger continued his research. Legend has it that one day, as his valet was powdering his wig, the chemist noticed that a new powder he could not identify was being used. Curious as to the origins of this unknown substance, he learnt that the supplier had by chance come upon a fine white mud in the countryside and had had the idea of turning it into powder for wigs. This mud was none other than the purest kaolin. Böttger incorporated it into his experiments and a year later was able to inform the Elector that he had mastered the making of hard paste porcelain, using a 'clay' mixed from kaolin, feldspar and various mineral binding agents. The first, or 'biscuit' firing gives a fine-grained matt surface which is then rendered smooth and glossy by the addition of a glaze composed of quartz feldspar, with or without gypsum added. Unlike soft paste glaze, that used for hard paste porcelain contains neither lead nor tin. The second firing is at 1400°C, ensuring the complete vitrification of the porcelain and the glaze. Certain types of statuette, however, are left at the biscuit stage.

It seems that in England the first soft paste porcelain was made in about 1745 in Chelsea, London, at a factory belonging to Nicholas Sprimont. A factory in Bow opened shortly afterwards and developed a stronger type of body, but the manufacture of true

This design has been copied from one used at the Royal Berlin porcelain works.

Hints on technique
Before you can paint flower patterns, you must learn to draw them. These examples are a useful way of getting acquainted with the basic shapes, pen-drawing technique and the use of colour.

porcelain in Britain had to await the establishment of William Cookworthy's factory in Plymouth in 1768. Cookworthy moved to Bristol in 1770. Other major British porcelain manufacturing centres were Liverpool, Swinton, Pinxton, Derby, New Hall, Coalport, Worcester and Swansea, to name but a few.

KEY NAMES

Böttger: At the beginning of the 18th century, the young German chemist and alchemist Johann Friedrich Böttger was led by his search for the philosopher's stone to the recipe for 'true porcelain'.

Augustus the Strong: Elector of Saxony, Böttger's patron and founder of Germany's first 'true porcelain' factory, at Meissen.

TECHNICAL TERMS

Soft paste: Type of chinaware made without kaolin and fired at a lower temperature than true porcelain.

Hard paste: Technical term for the kaolin mixture used for true porcelain.

'Medici Porcelain': Soft paste 16th-century Italian porcelain, now extremely rare.

THE GERMAN TRADITION: MEISSEN

When Johannes Böttcher announced his discovery of the method of making true porcelain (see pp. 43-46), his patron, Augustus the Strong, was as happy as if he had been presented with the philosopher's stone. The Elector's canny reaction, however, was to make the discovery public without releasing the smallest detail concerning the materials and techniques involved. Böttger's laboratory and the workshops were soon transferred to the fortress at Albrechtsberg, not far from the village of Meissen, near Dresden. This high-security setting had numerous advantages, in particular that of making it all but impossible for the workers to flee elsewhere. This was a common form of industrial self-protection at the time: the Republic of Venice, for example, accorded the master glass-makers of Murano all sorts of privileges, including astonishingly high wages, but the death penalty awaited those caught attempting to leave.

Working conditions at Meissen were excellent and the Elector offered full legal and financial indemnity to foreign craftsmen willing to enter the factory. In 1736 a fund was set up to help families in the event of a death and a second fund, established 20 years later, catered to the needs of workers' widows.

The division of labour was pushed to its limits at Meissen and certain pieces passed through the hands of many artists, each of whom had a highly specific task demanding the utmost care. The master craftsmen acted as overseers. Böttger himself had the title of 'Administrator', his main task being to ensure that the 'paste' and the glaze were up to standard - not an easy job in a field where the rulebook was still being written. The first pieces were shown at the Leipzig fair in 1710; they had numerous defects and in no way stood comparison with porcelain imported from China. When Böttger died in 1719, his place was taken by a group of overseers whose energy gave a rapid boost to the quality of the pieces and their decoration. The outcome was that in 1720 the Meissen works reached its goal of a high-temperature porcelain even whiter than the Chinese original. In the same year the management of the decoration workshop was entrusted to the brilliant young artist J.G.Höroldt, a master of traditional Chinese designs and the inventor of many others in the Chinese style. He set up a school

49

Flowers and insects in the Meissen style

of decoration whose best students were taken into the factory after an apprenticeship lasting six years. Those regarded as not up to standard were simply dismissed. At this time white porcelain fell into three categories, according to its quality. The first two groups - perfect pieces or those having minor defects that could be covered up - went on sale, while the markedly inferior pieces of the third category were made available to factory personnel on condition that they did not sell them. Unsurprisingly, this gave rise to an illicit decoration industry outside the factory and the combination of the defective items used, the carelessness of the decorative work and the low prices asked had an extremely bad effect on the image of the porcelain produced at Meissen. Almost all the major European manufacturers were badly affected by this practice, the

Vienna factory being particularly hard-hit. Something had to be done and in the second half of the 18th century appropriate measures were taken: defective pieces were either destroyed outright or marked in such a way as to prevent their being taken for the genuine article.

In 1731 Augustus the Strong emphasized the importance of the porcelain industry at Meissen by engaging the famous baroque-style modeller J.J. Kändler and taking a strong personal interest in the factory's administration and output; but after his death in 1733 his son, Augustus III, took a much less active role. From 1756 to 1763 Prussian troops occupied Meissen and plundered the workshops. Production ground to a halt as the craftsmen and workers dispersed into other factories. At this time Meissen's prestige was in tatters, its business having already been virtually wiped out by the craze for French porcelain and in particular by the rising star of Sèvres. Once production got under way again Meissen had to adapt to this new style, which in the meantime had swept Europe. The directors called in a French sculptor and designer, Jean-Michel Acier; a more than competent artist, Acier unfortunately lacked the

imagination and creative drive of Kändler, whose magnificent statuettes had helped make the factory's reputation. Kändler died in 1775, having just completed a sumptuous dinner service for Catherine the Great, Empress of Russia; and Acier retired in 1781. Although production at the factory went on apace (and continues to this day), the great era of Meissen was over and the name Dresden Porcelain is now often used to distinguish 19th century pieces from their illustrious predecessors.

> ### KEY NAMES
>
> **Meisen:** The factory in Germany which in 1720 succeeded in producing a true porcelain whiter than the Chinese original.
>
> **Dresden:** The name given to 19th-century Meissen porcelain to distinguish it from the output of the 18th-century 'golden age'.

The designs shown on this page come from a cocoa-jug made at Ansbach, site of one of the numerous small factories that sprang up in Germany in the 18th century. As we see from the treatment of the lid (below), the work is in two stages. First of all the design is blocked in (below left) using the minimum of colours and without any real attempt at subtlety. Then the shading and details are added (below right). The border pattern shows up black - the colour of gold before firing.

Birds in the Meissen style.

THE SECRET LEAKS OUT

In spite of the drastic measures taken at Meissen to protect the recipe for hard paste porcelain (see p.49), the secret could not be kept indefinitely. Rumour has it that Böttger took to drink towards the end of his life - he died in 1719 - and that his indiscretions were passed on by a certain Konrad Hunger to Claudius Innocentius Du Paquier, who had been trying various methods at his Vienna factory since 1717. Nevertheless, success eluded Du Paquier until he managed to obtain the services of Samuel Stölzel, a kiln-master who had fled the factory at Meissen. Hunger's colourful career as an industrial spy took a new turn when he quit Vienna in 1720 for Venice, where, with his help, Giovanni Vezzi set up the republic's first - and relatively shortlived - hard paste porcelain works, using kaolin illegally imported from Saxony. The ware produced by Vezzi was in general of Meissen standard. In 1727, however, the unpredictable Hunger found himself in financial difficulties that forced him to return to Meissen and denounce the illicit supplying of kaolin to the Venetian factory, which then closed. In Vienna, on the other hand, Du Paquier was prospering; the factory became a state establishment in 1744 and continued to produce elaborate, fine-quality tableware until its closure in 1866.

Leaks became more and more common towards the middle of the 18th century. Meissen continued to do its best to guard its many secrets, but little by little rival establishments sprang up, sometimes partially staffed by workers who for various reasons had made their escape from the pioneer factory.

A famous figure at this time was J.J. Ringler, a kind of roving porcelain specialist from Vienna. He played a part in the founding of numerous porcelain works in Germany, notably the Nymphenburg factory at Neudeck, near Munich, where the modeller Bustelli did for the rococo style what Kändler had done for the baroque. The factory at Nymphenburg remains in operation today and a part of its considerable output is still based on the original 18th century models.

Apart from renegade workers out to sell their knowledge to the highest bidder, the period was marked by the presence of numerous charlatans who travelled from one Court to another, claiming to know the secrets of porcelain making and decoration, but in fact only wasting the money of their credulous patrons. The possession of a porcelain works brought considerable prestige to its owner and its locality and the 18th century saw a veritable proliferation of such establishments in Europe, the main ones being Vienna (1719); Doccia, near Florence (1735), Vincennes, just outside Paris (1738); Capodimonte, near Naples (1743, transferred to a site near Madrid in 1759); Sèvres, near Paris (1756); Copenhagen (1759); the Royal German factory in Berlin (1763); and Plymouth (1768).

Pattern based on a Viennese porcelain design

A floral pattern that has survived the passing of time and countless changes of taste is this stylized cornflower, seen on the left-hand candlestick and adapted in different ways for the decoration of the drinking mugs on the opposite page. Tradition has it that the cornflower was the favourite design of Queen Marie-Antoinette of France.

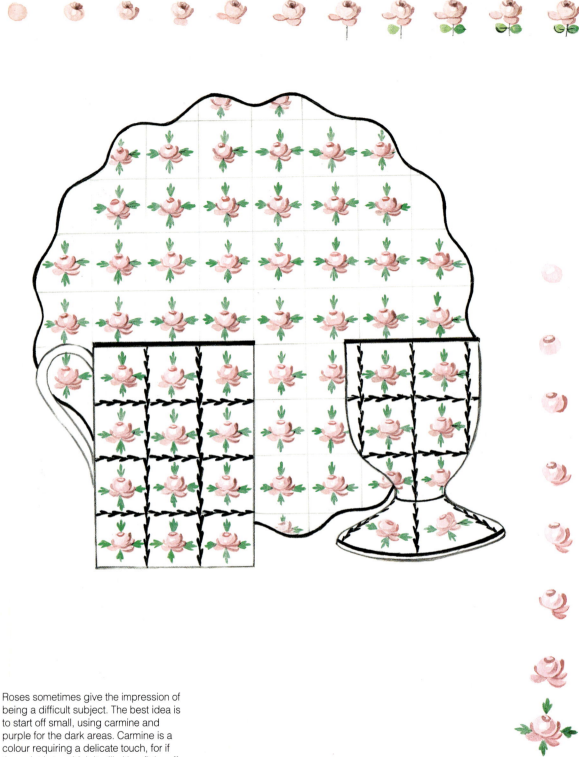

Roses sometimes give the impression of being a difficult subject. The best idea is to start off small, using carmine and purple for the dark areas. Carmine is a colour requiring a delicate touch, for if the paint is too thick it will either flake off or turn a sort of orange-brown during the firing. The design shown here, from the Herend works in Hungary, is excellent training for the artist's eye and hand.

Whatever the country and whatever the period, birds remain an unfailingly popular theme.

THE FRENCH MANNER: SEVRES

By the end of the 17th century French ceramicists had mastered the difficult art of soft paste manufacturing and learnt to maximise its beauty via the use of luminous lead-based glazes. In France the making of soft paste would continue in parallel with that of 'true' hard paste porcelain until just after 1800; during this time the factories at Saint-Cloud, Chantilly and Mennecy produced work of great beauty in terms of design and decoration. However, it was the hard paste factory at Sèvres, just outside Paris, that would come to overshadow the prestigious German establishment at Meissen and eventually dominate the European porcelain market.

In 1738 the Dubois brothers, two workers from the Chantilly soft paste works, were given permission to start a venture of their own and offered a workshop in the grounds of the Castle of Vincennes, near Paris. Despite this promising beginning the Dubois opted out of the project some four years later, leaving behind them, as luck would have it, Louis Gravant, another ex-Chantilly worker well-versed in the porcelain techniques of the time. A tireless and determined worker, Gravant got the Vincennes factory on its feet via imitations of pieces being made at Meissen.

In 1745 Charles Adam received

royal patronage for 'the making of porcelain in the Saxony style' at Vincennes and the factory became a larger-scale affair. Gravant's task, which he carried out admirably, was to improve the composition of the 'paste'. The staff at this time also included an expert in the preparation of porcelain paints and three specialist painters, two working on flowers and the third on birds and landscapes. Business flourished: a year later the factory was employing eighteen painters and by 1749 - the first year to see a substantial output of high-quality pieces - the total number of employees was 120. From 1750 onwards a chemist from the Academy of Sciences was called on to oversee the quality of the soft paste, the glazes and the decorative colours; management of the artistic side was entrusted to experienced painters.

Production costs, always a major problem, led to the winding-up of Adam's company and the establishment of another in which

Preliminary versions of Sèvres-style bouquets. The details of the flowers and leaves should only be added at the retouching stage.

67

the king, Louis XV, personally owned a quarter of the shares. In the meantime a porcelain-making venture at Sèvres headed by two artists, Bush and Stadelmayer, had ended in financial disaster. As it happened Madame de Pompadour, the king's mistress, was a passionate admirer of porcelain and persuaded the king to create a new factory at Sèvres, closer to the royal residence at Versailles. The building was completed in 1756 and the Vincennes workshop transferred there in the same year. A period of rapid expansion followed and two years later the factory had some 250 employees producing delicate soft paste ware - slender vases, long-necked jugs, ice buckets - of a typically French kind. The Meissen influence was limited to some of the decorative patterns used. Production costs remained a problem until 1759, when Louis XV bought the factory outright; Sèvres enjoyed royal protection until the execution of Louis XVI in 1791 and the factory is still in operation today.

The discovery of kaolin near Limoges in 1768 meant that Sèvres could undertake the manufacture of the hard paste porcelain pieces which would rapidly come to dominate the European market. The ware was characterized by rigorous design and production standards and an unrivalled use of colour. Nevertheless, copies proliferated and many English factories went in for large-scale imitation of Sèvres pieces.

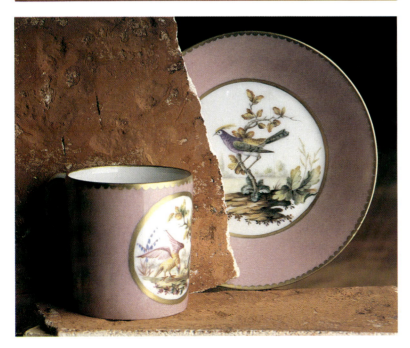

The background colour can be established by pouncing: this technique involves laying down the colour with a brush, then giving it uniformity by dabbing it lightly all over with a sponge or a special brush. The paints demand careful preparation: add mixing oil to the powder, follow up with a few drops of clove or lavender oil, then dilute with turpentine. Make it a rule to try out the consistency of the colour before painting and pouncing your backgrounds.

Sèvres: Shapes

The forms used at Sèvres during the reign of Louis XV are in the rococo style called rocaille, based on the convoluted shapes of seashells. The models were supplied by Louis XV's silversmith and were directly inspired by silverware pieces. A specialty at Sèvres was the making of vast table settings, for which orders flowed in from all over Europe. The most elaborate, supplied to Catherine the Great of Russia, cost £300 000.
Under Louis XVI (reigned 1774-1791) the shapes changed. The typical line became simpler and a trifle severe, but with no loss of elegance.

Decoration

Up until 1770 or thereabouts, European porcelain continued to be influenced, directly or otherwise, by Chinese and Japanese forms. Certain distinctively European models were conceived at Meissen and, in France, by the painter Fraisse, who had links with the factory at Chantilly. The fact that the factory at Vincennes, the direct predecessor of Sèvres, was founded by the Dubois brothers and Louis Gravant - all trained at Chantilly - explains the Meissen and Chantilly influences at the beginning, but neither Vincennes nor Sèvres went in for mere servile copying. Their adaptations of certain oriental designs show considerable originality and when we look at the highly individual use of dots, lines and elements in relief on Sèvres ware, we can be forgiven for not immediately identifying the sources of inspiration.

In the same way, the flowers and birds portrayed by hatching on Meissen were treated with a steadily increasing naturalism at Sèvres, where they came to typify the style. Flowers in particular are almost always present, even if their role is only a secondary one. The success of bird motifs, also much used at Sèvres, probably reflects the attachment to nature fashionable at the time. The Chinese pheasant is among the most frequently used, while a large proportion of the others are drawn from the illustrations of the great naturalist Georges Buffon (1707-1788). Marie-Antoinette's passion for peasant life also inspired numerous farm-yard scenes. But above all it is the use of coloured backgrounds - inimitable yellows, pinks, greens and blues - that sets Sèvres apart. These serve as a backdrop to cartouches showing pastoral, mythological and military scenes which are veritable paintings in their own right, even if copied from earlier originals. Framed by graceful rocaille outlines and flower-laden branches painted in gold relief, these designs allowed Sèvres to conquer the whole of Europe.

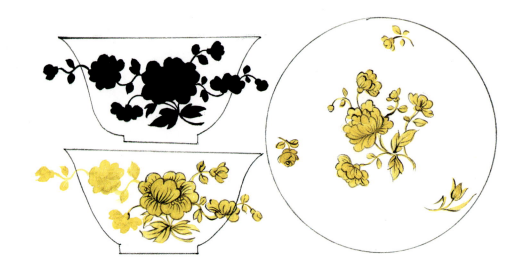

76

Evenness of coverage is essential to the success of all decorative work using gold paint. First of all, before starting work on the piece in question, give the design one or more trial runs using a normal colour. The homogeneity of gold paint is crucial at all times; the gold tends to form deposits in the bottom of the jar and needs to be stirred regularly - shaking is not enough. Gold paint has an inherent beauty that complements coloured backgrounds perfectly and, discriminatingly used, can be a most effective means of covering up mistakes in pouncing.